Rocks & Minerals

Grades 1–3

INVESTIGATING SCIENCE

Project Managers:
Irving P. Crump and Thad H. McLaurin

Writers:
Jan Brennan and Mary Sanford

Editors:
Cindy K. Daoust, Deborah T. Kalwat, Scott Lyons,
Leanne Stratton, Hope H. Taylor

Art Coordinator:
Clevell Harris

Artists:
Theresa Lewis Goode, Nick Greenwood, Clevell Harris,
Barry Slate, Donna K. Teal

Cover Artists:
Nick Greenwood and Kimberly Richard

www.themailbox.com

©2000 by THE EDUCATION CENTER, INC.
All rights reserved.
ISBN #1-56234-445-5

Manufactured in the United States

10 9 8 7 6 5 4 3 2

S0-DOP-728

Table of Contents

About This Book

Welcome to *Investigating Science—Rocks & Minerals*! This book is one of ten must-have resource books that support the National Science Education Standards and are designed to supplement and enhance your existing science curriculum. Packed with practical cross-curricular ideas and thought-provoking reproducibles, these all-new, content-specific resource books provide primary teachers with a collection of innovative and fun activities for teaching thematic science units.

Included in this book:

Investigating Science—Rocks & Minerals contains six cross-curricular thematic units each containing
- Background information for the teacher
- Easy-to-implement instructions for science experiments and projects
- Student-centered activities and reproducibles
- Literature links

Cross-curricular thematic units found in this book:
- *Characteristics of Rocks and Minerals*
- *The Three Types of Rocks*
- *The Rock Cycle*
- *Uses of Rocks and Minerals*
- *Sand and Soil*
- *Famous and Unusual Rocks*

Other books in the primary Investigating Science series:
- *Investigating Science—Amphibians & Reptiles*
- *Investigating Science—Environment*
- *Investigating Science—Solar System*
- *Investigating Science—Insects*
- *Investigating Science—Energy, Light, & Sound*
- *Investigating Science—Plants*
- *Investigating Science—Weather*
- *Investigating Science—Mammals*
- *Investigating Science—Health & Safety*

Characteristics of Rocks and Minerals

Ensure a solid introduction to rocks and minerals with these polished activities and reproducibles.

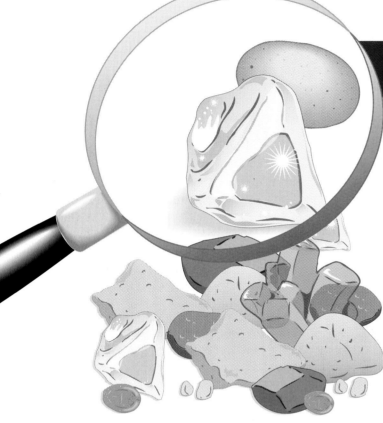

Digging Into Rocks
(Collecting Rocks)

Your rock hunters will be eager to gather collections of rocks for this craggy exploration unit! In advance, have each student collect rocks of different sizes (no bigger than a fist), shapes, and colors from around his home and neighborhood and bring them to school. On a designated day, have students share their rock collections with the class; then brainstorm a list of rock characteristics, such as *heavy, light, rough, smooth, shiny, dull, big,* and *little.* Label several rock-shaped cutouts with the characteristics from the class-generated list. Pair up the characteristics (heavy and light, etc.) and place each pair of cutouts in a different location in the classroom. Divide students into small groups and then have them sort their rocks onto pairs of labeled cutouts. After several minutes, have each group move to the next pair of cutouts and re-sort the rocks. Continue this process until each group has visited each pair of characteristics.

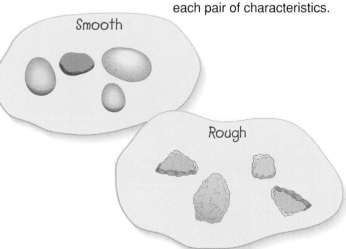

Background for the Teacher

- The solid part of the earth is called *rock.*
- Rocks are found under soil, water, and polar ice caps.
- Rocks are made up of *minerals.* Most rocks are aggregates (combinations) of minerals.
- A rock can have one or more colors depending on the mineral(s) present.
- The *hardness* of a mineral is tested by scratching one mineral with another.
- The *streak* test uses color to determine a mineral type. The streak color can differ from the actual color of the mineral.
- A simple acid test can determine the presence of limestone.
- All *gems* come from rocks except pearl, amber, and coral.
- The millions of tiny holes in *pumice* make it possible for this rock to float on water.

Books That Rock

Is There a Dinosaur in Your Backyard? by Spencer Christian and Antonia Felix (John Wiley & Sons, Inc.; 1998)

Milo and the Magical Stones by Marcus Pfister (North-South Books Inc., 1997)

My Ol' Man by Patricia Polacco (PaperStar, 1999)

Rock Talk
(Vocabulary)

Acquaint your youngsters with some rock lingo with this vocabulary activity. Explain to students that discovering the characteristics of rocks can help in identifying them. Discuss each rock term in the box with students; then have them make self-checking vocabulary cards. Supply each student with the materials listed below; then have him follow the steps to complete the project.

Materials needed for each student:
1 tagboard copy of page 8
scissors
6' length of thin string
1 bead
access to tape and a hole puncher

Steps:
1. Cut your paper along the dashed line at the bottom of the page.
2. Fold the paper in half along the fold line.
3. Tape the edges of the paper together opposite the fold.
4. Hole-punch where indicated.
5. Tie one end of the string to the bead.
6. Starting from the back of the card, thread the string through the hole next to the first vocabulary word on the left side. Then thread the string through the hole next to the matching definition on the right side.
7. Continue this process with each vocabulary word and definition, working from top to bottom.
8. Check the back of the card to see if your string overlaps the lines on the card correctly.

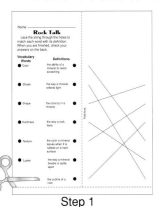
Step 1

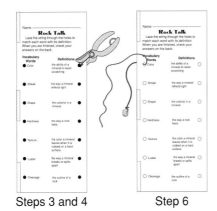
Steps 3 and 4   Step 6

color—the color or colors present in the mineral
luster—the way a mineral reflects light; lusters include shiny, dull, sparkly, and metallic
texture—the way a rock feels; textures include smooth, rough, coarse, grainy, and jagged
shape—the outline of the rock
streak—the color a mineral leaves when it is rubbed on a hard surface; streaks reveal the true color of the rock
hardness—the ability of a rock to resist scratching
cleavage—the way a mineral breaks or splits apart; minerals can make a clean break, form into cubes, make jagged edges, or make shell-like shapes

(Front)   (Back)

Rock Reports
(Making a Booklet)

It's time to get down to the nitty-gritty of rock exploration! Instruct each child to make a rock report booklet in which to record data. Distribute the materials listed below; then have each student follow the steps to complete her booklet. Have students complete the activities on pages 6 and 7 of this unit and record their findings in the booklets.

Materials needed for each student:
1 copy each of pages 9, 10, and 11
scissors
1/2 of a resealable snack bag with the cut side taped closed as shown
access to a stapler
1 small rock

Steps:
1. Cut the booklet pages along the dashed lines.
2. Stack the pages in order; then staple them along the left side.
3. Open the resealable bag and staple one thickness of it to the cover of the booklet below the words *My Rock Report.*
4. Place the selected rock in the bag.
5. Complete the booklet pages after visiting each rock-testing center.

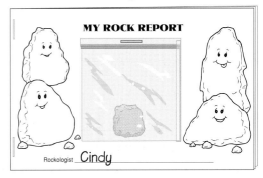
MY ROCK REPORT
Rockologist Cindy

Set up the experiments below and on page 7 in centers around your classroom. Have your rock hounds visit the centers and gather remarkable rock data to complete their booklet pages.

Take a Closer Look

Encourage students to take a good look at rock specimens with this simple activity. Place a pan of water, small scrub brushes, paper towels, and several hand lenses in a center. Direct each child to scrub his rock clean and then dry it using a paper towel. Next, instruct the child to look at his rock through a hand lens. After he has carefully inspected the rock, have the child illustrate it on page 1 of his booklet and complete the sentences on the page. What an eye for details!

True Colors

Help students discover the true color of a rock by performing a streak test. This test is one way of identifying the mineral(s) present in a rock. In advance, gather several unglazed ceramic tiles. Have each student rub her rock across a tile. Explain to students that a small amount of the rock is ground as the rock is moved across the tile. The streak of color left on the tile's surface is the rock's true color. (If no colored streak is left, the rock is harder than the tile.) Next, direct each student to use the information gathered during the streak test to complete page 2 of her booklet.

Hard Evidence

Students can scratch the surface and learn about rock hardness with this activity. Explain to students that in 1822 Friedrich Mohs developed a scale to measure the hardness of minerals. The Mohs scale lists ten minerals from softest (talc) to hardest (diamond). A mineral will scratch other minerals softer than itself and will be scratched by minerals that are harder. Have students determine the hardness of their rocks with this simplified test. Place pennies, old table knives, and a couple of glass jars in a center. Have each student try to scratch a penny, a knife, and a glass jar with his rock; then have him color the pictures of the objects that his rock scratched on page 3 of his booklet. Next, direct the child to scratch his rock with his fingernail, a penny, and a knife and then color the pictures of the objects that scratched the rock. Have the child use the data he collected during the scratch test to complete the sentences on page 3.

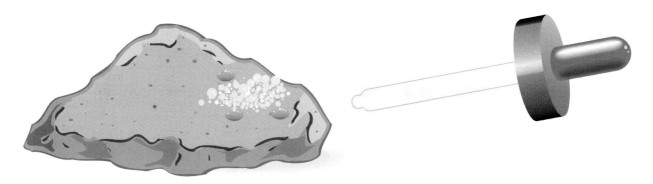

Fizzy Findings

As students collect information from this experiment, they'll learn more about the identification of rocks. Explain to students that rocks containing limestone will *effervesce,* or bubble, when they come in contact with a weak acid such as vinegar. Place a container of vinegar, droppers, and paper towels in a center. Instruct each child to use the dropper to drop a small amount of the vinegar onto her rock. Have the child carefully observe the rock and look for bubbling where the vinegar touched it. *(A rock that doesn't effervesce does not contain limestone.)* Instruct each child to record her findings on page 4 of her booklet. Drip, drip, fizz, fizz!

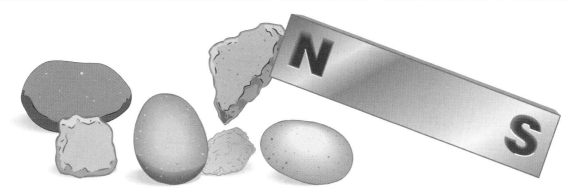

Attractive Rocks

Students cling to this activity to see if their rocks have the property of magnetism. In advance, gather several magnets and place them in a center. Explain to youngsters that a rock containing metal will be attracted to a magnet. Direct each child to touch his rock to a magnet and observe whether he feels magnetic attraction between the two objects. Have each student record his findings on page 5 of his booklet.

Get Wet!

It's time for rocks to take a dip! Set up a center containing a bucket of water and paper towels. Have each youngster drop her rock into the water and observe whether it floats on top of the water or sinks to the bottom of the bucket. (Pumice will float on water.) Direct each child to complete page 5 of her booklet by recording the data gathered from this test.

Name _____

Rock Talk

Lace the string through the holes to match each word with its definition. When you are finished, check your answers on the back.

Vocabulary Words	**Definitions**

● Color

● Streak

● Shape

● Hardness

● Texture

● Luster

● Cleavage

● the ability of a mineral to resist scratching

● the way a mineral reflects light

● the color(s) in a mineral

● the way a rock feels

● the color a mineral leaves when it is rubbed on a hard surface

● the way a mineral breaks or splits apart

● the outline of a rock

Fold here.

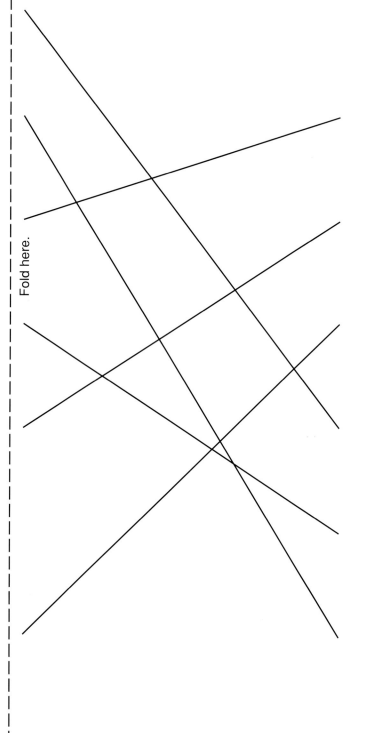

Note to the teacher: Use with "Rock Talk" on page 5.

MY ROCK REPORT

Rockologist _____

Take a Closer Look

This is a picture of my rock.

My rock's color is _____

_____.

My rock's texture is _____

_____.

I found my rock _____

_____

_____.

1

True Colors

☐ My rock did not leave a streak.

☐ My rock did leave a streak.

The streak color was _____.

My rock streak color looked like this:

2

Hard Evidence

My rock scratched a _____.

A _____ scratched my rock.

My rock is harder than a _____

and softer than a _____.

3

Note to the teacher: Use with "Rock Reports" on page 5.

Fizzy Findings

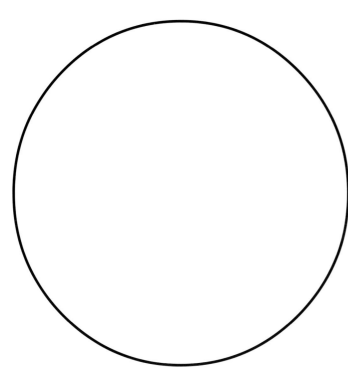

My rock looked like this when I put vinegar on it.

My rock _____ fizz.
(did or did not)

My rock _____
(does or does not)
contain limestone.

4

Attractive Rocks

My rock _____ cling to a magnet.
(did or did not)

I learned _____

_____

_____.

Get Wet!

My rock _____.
(sinks or floats)

Note to the teacher: Use with "Rock Reports" on page 5.

The Three Types of Rocks

Dig into these fun and informative ideas, activities, and reproducibles to teach your students about the three types of rocks.

Background for the Teacher

- The earth's crust is made up of three types of rocks: *igneous, sedimentary,* and *metamorphic.*
- The word *igneous* means "made by heat."
- Igneous rock is formed when melted rock, called *magma,* pushes through cracks in the earth's crust in the form of *lava* and then cools and solidifies.
- *Granite, pumice, obsidian,* and *basalt* are types of igneous rock.
- The word *sedimentary* comes from a word that means "to settle."
- Sedimentary rocks are layered rocks. They are formed when weathered and eroded rock pieces, called *sediment,* are deposited in layers that become buried and compressed. Over time the different rock particles become cemented together, forming new sedimentary rocks.
- *Shale, sandstone,* and *limestone* are types of sedimentary rock.
- Fossils are often found within the layers of sedimentary rocks.
- *Metamorphic* comes from the Greek words *meta* and *morphe,* and means "change of form."
- Metamorphic rocks are formed when igneous or sedimentary rocks are changed by heat or pressure or both.
- *Quartzite, marble,* and *slate* are types of metamorphic rocks.

A Collection of Rock Books

The Best Book of Fossils, Rocks, and Minerals by Chris Pellant (Larousse Kingfisher Chambers Inc., 2000)

The Magic School Bus: Inside the Earth by Joanna Cole (Scholastic Inc., 1989)

On My Beach There Are Many Pebbles by Leo Lionni (Mulberry Books, 1995)

Rocks & Minerals (The Wonders of Our World series) by Neil Morris (Crabtree Publishing Company, 1998)

The Worry Stone by Marianna Dengler (Northland Publishing Company, 1996)

Introducing...Rocks!
(Listening, Processing Information)

Rock on with your study of the three types of rocks with this scrambled sentence activity! Begin by reading aloud *Let's Go Rock Collecting* by Roma Gans (HarperCollins Children's Books, 1997). Also share with your students the facts found in "Background for the Teacher" on this page. Next, provide a copy of page 17 for each student. Have him cut out each word in scrambled sentence number 1. Then instruct him to arrange the words in the correct order and glue them in place in the appropriate box at the top of page 17. Invite him to take his completed page home to share his rockin' new knowledge with his family.

Three types of rocks

Name __Matt__

Scrambled Rock Sentences

Igneous rock forms when magma cools and hardens.

Basalt is the most common igneous rock.

Sedimentary rock forms from layers of sediment.

Sandstone is one type of sedimentary rock.

Metamorphic rock forms when rocks are changed by heat and/or pressure.

Marble is a type of metamorphic rock.

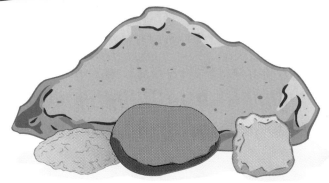

A Rock Reference
(Making a Booklet)

Provide a solid rock reference for students with this booklet-making project. Furnish the materials listed and guide students through the steps shown to make their own rock reference booklets. Copy the information found in "Background for the Teacher" on page 12 onto chart paper to post in the classroom, or give each student a photocopy of the information. Have each child refer to this information and other reference materials to complete her booklet.

Materials for each student:
one 4¹/₂" x 12" piece of colored construction paper
1 copy of page 18
1 copy of page 19
reference books about rocks (see the list on page 12)
glue
scissors
crayons

Steps:
1. Cut out the three booklet pages and the three rock formation cards.
2. Read each card; then glue it to the top of the matching booklet page.
3. Using a book about rocks as a reference, color the rocks on each booklet page.
4. Stack the booklet pages.
5. Fold the construction paper to make a booklet cover. Slip the stacked pages inside the cover and staple along the left-hand side.
6. Title your booklet "A Rock Reference." Write your name on the cover, and then decorate the cover as desired.

Igneous Rock Candy
(Experiment)

For a delicious hands-on look at the formation of igneous rocks, try making some igneous rock candy! Place in a glass mixing bowl one tablespoon of chocolate or butterscotch morsels for each student in the class. Microwave the morsels on high for 20 seconds or until they are melted and can be stirred with a spoon. Display in front of your students a handful of unmelted chips next to the bowl of melted chips. Next, invite a student volunteer to stir the melted chip mixture and comment on its texture and consistency. Then have each child, in turn, spoon a dollop of the melted chips onto a small piece of waxed paper. As the "rocks" cool, ask students to apply their knowledge of igneous rock formation to the experiment and discuss the similarities. *(Igneous rock is formed when melted rock, called magma, pushes through cracks in the earth's crust in the form of lava and then cools and solidifies.)* Once the liquid treat has cooled and hardened, invite each child to gobble up his igneous rock!

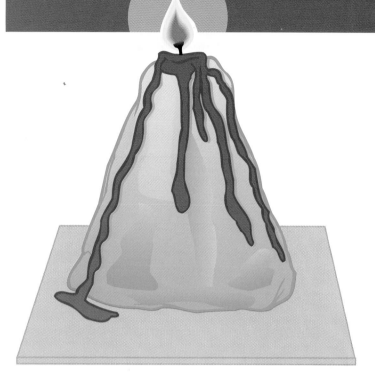

A Candle Volcano
(Demonstration)

Viewing a compact candle volcano is a safe way for students to learn more about igneous rocks. To make the volcano, use a sharp knife to cut three inches off the top of a tapered dinner candle. (Be sure not to use dripless candles.) Mold a handful of clay into a pliable ball and insert the three-inch candle into the center of the ball. Form the clay around the candle into a volcano. Then press the clay around the candle until only the tip is visible. Direct students to gather in a circle a safe distance from the volcano. Then light the candle and have the students observe the wax as it melts and drips down the side of the clay. After some wax has pooled around the bottom of the volcano, extinguish the flame and allow the wax to cool. Then pass the volcano around for students to examine. Explain to students that the dripping candle wax is like the hot liquid rock that spews out of a volcano in the form of lava onto the earth's surface. The liquid rock, called *lava,* cools and hardens to form igneous rock similar to the hardened candle wax.

The Metamorphic Mash
(Experiment)

For a quick and meaningful lesson about the change that pressure can make on rocks, try this smashing demonstration! Remind students that one way a metamorphic rock is formed is by applying pressure to two different rocks so that they change and become one rock. To demonstrate this phenomenon, divide the class into groups, provide the materials listed, and guide each group through the steps shown.

Materials for each group:
two 6" x 6" squares of 1"-thick quilt batting
1 hardcover textbook or dictionary
1 ruler
1 sheet of white paper for each child
pencils

Steps:
1. Place the pieces of quilt batting side by side on the table. On a sheet of paper, draw a picture of the batting and write a short description of its appearance.
2. Stack the two pieces; then use the ruler to measure the height of the stack. Draw the stack and write a short description of it.
3. Place the book on top of the stack so that one edge of the batting is showing. Have one group member press down on the book with both hands. Direct another member to measure the height of the visible edge of the batting.
4. Write and illustrate a description of the change that the pressure from the book is causing in the batting.
5. Explain how this demonstration is similar to the formation of a metamorphic rock.

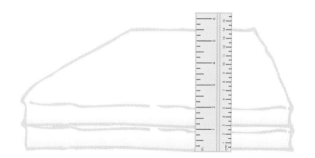

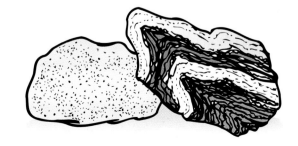

Metamorphic Gumdrops
(Experiment)

Have your students make a tasty metamorphic treat with the following activity. In advance, purchase several bags of gumdrops and use sharp scissors to carefully cut each gumdrop into three pieces. Give each child two 5" x 5" squares of waxed paper and 12 to 15 gumdrop pieces of assorted colors. Have the child pile his gumdrop pieces in the center of one waxed paper square. Then instruct him to lay the second square on top of the pile and use his palm to press down on the gumdrop pieces for several seconds. Direct the child to peel the wax paper off to reveal his colorful metamorphic rock. Explain to your students that, in the same manner, rocks can be changed into new rocks by the weight of the earth's layers pressing down on them.

Layers Upon Layers
(Experiment)

You're sure to build understanding of the layering process of sedimentary rocks with this group experiment! After reviewing the formation process of sedimentary rocks (see the background information on page 12), give each group the materials listed below. Guide the group through the steps shown to make a model of layers of sediment. As the experiment progresses, provide time for each group to share their observations with the class at each stage of the experiment.

Materials for each group:
1 quart jar with lid
1 clean, empty widemouthed jar
$^1/_2$ c. flour
$^1/_2$ c. dry rice
$^1/_2$ c. dry pinto beans
2 c. of tap water

Steps:
1. Pour one cup of water into the quart jar and add the beans, rice, and flour. Then add the second cup of water.
2. Tightly screw the lid onto the jar and take turns shaking the contents vigorously for five to ten minutes.
3. Pour the contents into the widemouthed jar. Watch the contents and write your observations on a sheet of paper.
4. Examine the contents every 15 minutes for an hour. Continue to note your observations. *(The water will be cloudy until the mixture begins to settle. As it settles, three layers will become visible: a layer of beans and rice, a layer of flour, and a layer of dirty-looking water. Some of the flour will drift down to fill in the spaces in the layer of rice and beans.)*
5. Leave the jar in an undisturbed place overnight. Examine the jar the next day and record your observations.

Sedimentary Cementation
(Demonstration)

What's the glue that helps hold sedimentary rocks together? The answer can be found in a drop of water! Give students an up close view of the dissolved minerals that a drop of water usually contains with this demonstration! Use an eyedropper to make a puddle of tap water on a 4" square of clear plastic. Leave the square in an undisturbed place for three to five days or until the water evaporates. Hold the square up to a sunny window and examine the minerals that are left on the plastic. If desired, repeat the experiment with bottled water or water samples from other sources. Then compare the minerals left by tap water with the minerals left by other samples. Explain to students that as water passes through the layers of sediment, the minerals act as glue helping cement the layers together.

Sandstone Sample
(Experiment)

Give students a firsthand view of cementation in action with this sedimentary rock activity. Remind students that sedimentary rocks are formed when tiny pieces of rock and other materials are compressed and bound together. Provide each student with the materials listed and guide her through the steps shown to help her make a sandstone sample.

Materials for each child:
$1/2$ c. sand
$1/2$ c. water
3 tbsp. Epsom salts
two 9-oz. paper cups
1 spoon

Steps:
1. Pour the sand into one cup.
2. Pour the water and the Epsom salts into the second cup. Stir the mixture for three minutes or until the salt is dissolved.
3. Pour the water mixture over the sand.
4. After five minutes have passed, carefully pour off any water that has accumulated on the sand.
5. Repeat Step 4 until water no longer accumulates.
6. Place the cup in an undisturbed place for seven to ten days. Then gently tip the cup until the mixture drops out. If it is still wet, return it to the undisturbed place until it is dry. When the mixture is dry, examine the sandstones that have formed.

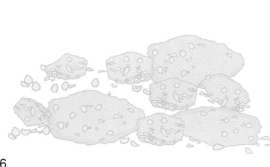

Scrambled Rock Sentences

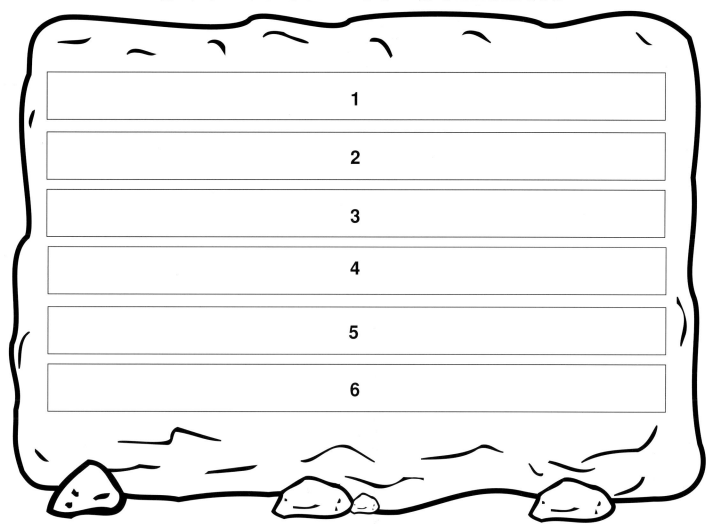

1	forms	Igneous	cools	rock	and	hardens.	magma	when			
2	most	is	Basalt	igneous	the	rock.	common				
3	layers	from	sediment.	rock	Sedimentary	forms	of				
4	type	rock.	Sandstone	of	one	sedimentary	is				
5	pressure.	rocks	forms	heat	are	Metamorphic	when	by	and/or	rock	changed
6	type	rock.	is	metamorphic	Marble	a	of				

Note to the teacher: Use with "Introducing…Rocks!" on page 12.

Patterns

Use with "A Rock Reference" on page 13.

Igneous Rock

Igneous Rock

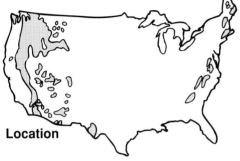

Location

Facts About Igneous Rock

- There are two classifications of igneous rock: *extrusive* and *intrusive.*
- Extrusive rock forms on the earth's surface.
- Intrusive rock forms beneath the earth's surface.

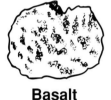   

Basalt　　**Pumice**　　**Obsidian**　　**Granite**

©2000 The Education Center, Inc. • *Investigating Science* • *Rocks & Minerals* • TEC1747

Metamorphic Rock

Metamorphic Rock

Location

Facts About Metamorphic Rock

- Granite can be changed into gneiss.
- Limestone can be changed into marble.
- Sandstone can be changed into quartzite.

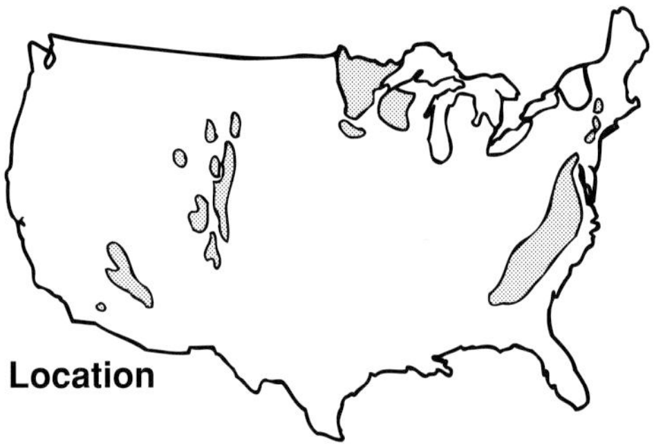

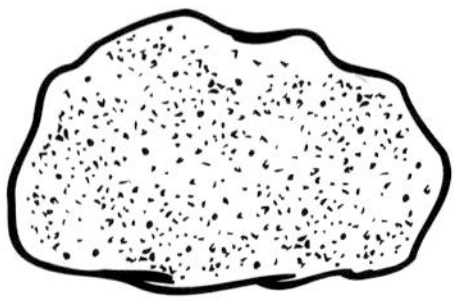

Marble 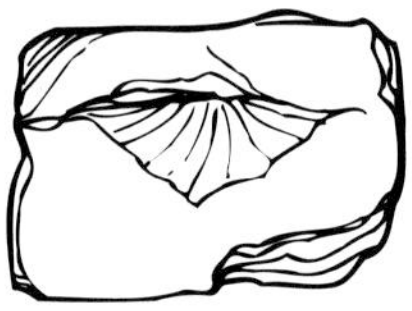　　**Slate**　　**Quartzite**　　**Gneiss**

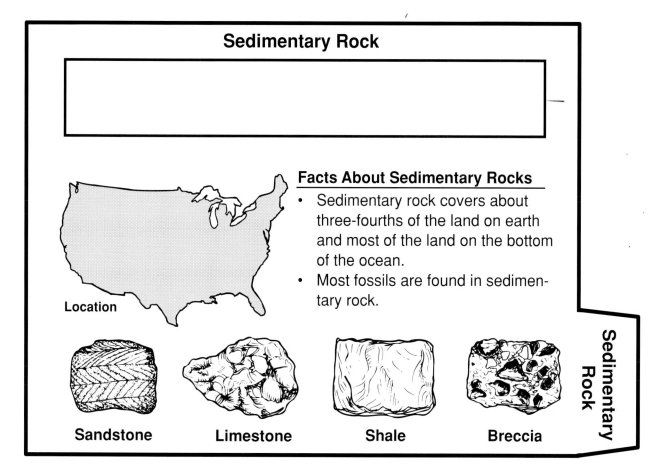

Sedimentary Rock

Facts About Sedimentary Rocks
- Sedimentary rock covers about three-fourths of the land on earth and most of the land on the bottom of the ocean.
- Most fossils are found in sedimentary rock.

Location

Sandstone   Limestone   Shale   Breccia

Sedimentary Rock

Rock Formation Cards

This type of rock forms when heat or pressure or both cause changes in the other two types of rock.
This type of rock forms when molten material, or magma, cools and hardens.
This type of rock forms when small pieces of clay, silt, or sand settle into layers on the bottoms of lakes and oceans. The pressure of the water and the layers above compress the pieces into rock.

The Rock Cycle

Round and round they go! Introduce your students to the never-ending rock cycle with this collection of hands-on activities.

Background for the Teacher

- Rocks change from one type to another through a never-ending process called the *rock cycle.*
- No matter how hard it is, a rock will eventually be broken down.
- All rocks come from other rocks.
- When sedimentary or metamorphic rock melts and then cools, *igneous rock* is formed.
- *Sedimentary rock* is made from broken pieces of metamorphic or igneous rock. These pieces are caused by weathering, then deposited in layers. The layers are compacted and cemented together.
- Heat and pressure can change igneous or sedimentary rock into *metamorphic rock.*
- *Weathering* is when the sun, wind, water, plants, or animals wear away rocks, breaking them into smaller pieces. *Erosion* is the moving of these small pieces from one place to another by wind or water.
- Scientists learn how the earth is changing by studying rocks and how they recycle.

The Book Mine

Discover Rocks & Minerals by Joel E. Arem (Publications International, 1991)
The Earth & Beyond by Chris Oxlade (Heineman Library, 1998)
Janice VanCleave's A+ Projects in Earth Science: Winning Experiments for Science Fairs and Extra Credit by Janice VanCleave (John Wiley & Sons, Inc.; 1998)
Planet Earth (Time-Life Student Library) edited by Jean Crawford (Time Life, 1999)
Rocks & Fossils (Nature Company Guide) edited by Arthur Busbey (Time Life, 1996)

Rockin' With the Rock Cycle
(Study Guide)

Help your students understand the key points of the rock cycle with a study guide. Duplicate page 23 for each child. Begin a discussion of the rock cycle by explaining to students that all rocks—no matter what type they are, how hard they are, or where they are found—will be broken down by a variety of forces and changed into other types of rock.

Display a sample of each of the three types of rocks for students to observe. (See the arrows below for some suggestions.) Hold up one of the rocks, identify it, and tell what type it is. Then tell students that it can be changed into another rock type through millions of years of natural forces. Next, refer students to the reproducible and have them complete it according to the directions.

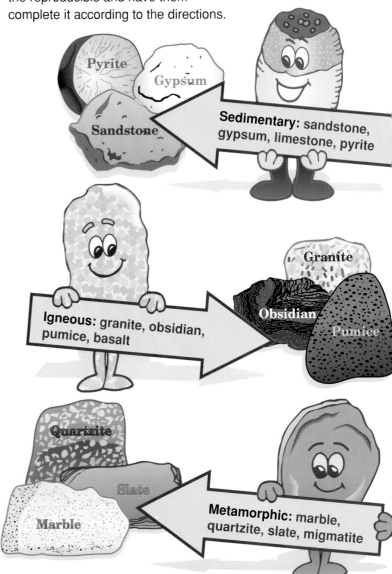

Pyrite
Gypsum
Sandstone
Sedimentary: sandstone, gypsum, limestone, pyrite

Granite
Obsidian
Pumice
Igneous: granite, obsidian, pumice, basalt

Quartzite
Slate
Marble
Metamorphic: marble, quartzite, slate, migmatite

Rock Out!
(Simulation Game)

Get students up and moving with this game that simulates the rock cycle. In advance, cut an equal number of red, blue, and brown rock shapes from construction paper so that each student will have a rock. Randomly distribute the rocks to students, one per child. Explain that the red rocks are *igneous,* the blue ones *sedimentary,* and the brown ones *metamorphic.* Choose three volunteers to bring their rocks to the front of the class.

When you say, "Heads down, rocks out!", all students who are seated put their rocks on their desks, close their eyes, and put their heads down. The three volunteers then circulate around the classroom, exchange their rocks with three students who are seated, and return to the front of the room. Next, call out, "Heads up, rocks check!" at which time each seated student checks his rock to see if it has changed. The three students who now have different rocks stand up. If each one can state the change and why it happened, he takes the place of the student who exchanged rocks with him. If not, he sits back down. For example: If a student began with a metamorphic rock (brown) and it changed to an igneous rock (red), he must say that his metamorphic rock was changed by heat and pressure.

Keep rockin' until everyone has had a turn being a part of the rock cycle!

My rock changed from brown *(metamorphic)* to red *(igneous)*. My rock was changed by heat and pressure.

A long, long, long, long, long time ago...

If Rocks Could Talk
(Writing, Illustrating)

Oh, the stories they could tell...if only rocks could talk! In advance, ask each student to bring a small to medium-sized rock to class. As a class, try to identify each rock and determine whether it's sedimentary, igneous, or metamorphic. Review with students that the rock cycle is an ongoing process: Slowly, over millions of years, rocks are broken down and then reformed. Further explain that at one time, any rock now sitting on a student's desk could have been at the top of a mountain or covered by the sea. And that rock has a story to tell!

Brainstorm a list of changes that could occur in the rock cycle. Then have each student write a rough draft of the story of his rock, including how it changed to its current form. Have students give their rocks personalities by using markers and paints to add facial features, hair, glasses, etc. Display the final versions of these "rock-umentaries" on a table along with the rock personalities.

Sweet Changes!
(Group Experiment)

Students get a close-up look at how rocks change with this hands-on activity!

Materials needed for each group of three students:

3 zippered sandwich bags: 1 containing 10 regular chocolate chips, 1 with 10 white chocolate chips, and 1 with 10 butterscotch chips
two 8" strips of waxed paper
plastic knife
zippered sandwich bag
small plastic cup
hot and cold tap water
ice cubes (optional)

STEP 2

Steps:

1. Divide students into groups of three and give each group the three bags of candy chips and the waxed paper strips. Each student selects a bag of candy chips. *(The chips represent small rocks and minerals.)*

2. With each bag securely sealed, direct each student to gently work the candy rocks and minerals between his hands until they combine into a single rock. *(This represents how pieces of rocks join together under pressure and heat to form metamorphic rock.)*

3. The student with the regular chocolate chip rock opens his bag and places his rock on a sheet of waxed paper. He covers his rock with the second sheet of waxed paper, then presses down to form a flat layer. He then removes the top sheet of waxed paper.

4. The student with the white chocolate chip rock opens his bag and places his rock on top of the first layer. He then re-covers the two rocks with the sheet of waxed paper and presses them together. He then removes the waxed paper.

5. The student with the butterscotch rock repeats the procedure to make a third layer.

6. Next, have a student in each group cut and divide the rock into two sections. Have students observe the three distinct layers. *(This represents the way layers of rocks pile up. Over thousands of years, pressure causes them to form sedimentary rock.)*

7. Have a student cut the layered rocks into small pieces and place them in a zippered bag. With the bag securely sealed, have the student put it in the plastic cup. Pour hot tap water into the cup and allow it to sit for five minutes. Have students examine the bag. *(The heat melts the rock, which represents magma.)*

8. Have a student in each group pour out the hot water and then refill the cup with cold tap water and an ice cube, if available. Allow the bag to sit in the cold water for about five minutes. *(The magma will harden to represent igneous rock.)*

9. Next, have a student break the igneous rock into small pieces. *(This represents weathering. Tell students that the rock cycle then starts all over!)*

STEP 6

STEP 8

Rockin' With the Rock Cycle

Use a word from the rock pile to complete each sentence.

1. _____ rock forms when melted rock cools and then hardens.

2. _____ rock forms when layers of sediment bond together.

3. _____ rock forms when pressure or heat changes rock.

metamorphic   igneous   sedimentary

Complete the rock cycle.

1. Write each of the following sentences in the correct outer arrow:
   • Layers of sediment join together.
   • Melted rock cools and hardens.
   • Changes are made by heat and pressure.

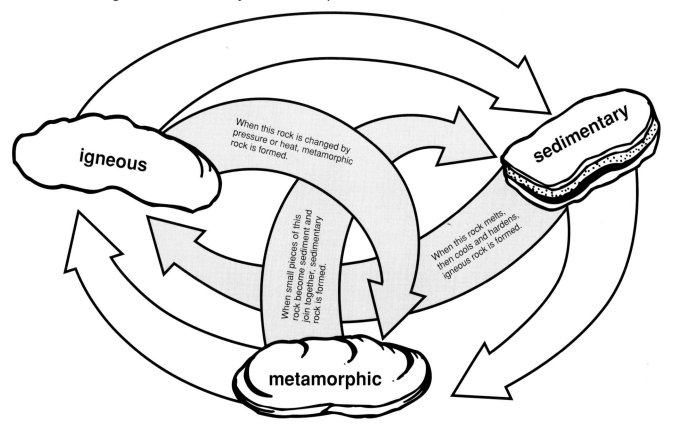

igneous

sedimentary

When this rock is changed by pressure or heat, metamorphic rock is formed.

When this rock melts, then cools and hardens, igneous rock is formed.

When small pieces of this rock become sediment and join together, sedimentary rock is formed.

metamorphic

2. Lightly color the outer arrow pointing to igneous rock red.
3. Lightly color the outer arrow pointing to sedimentary rock blue.
4. Lightly color the outer arrow pointing to metamorphic rock brown.

Uses of Rocks and Minerals

Your students will dig these ideas, activities, and reproducibles on the different uses of rocks and minerals.

Everyday Minerals
(Researching, Observing, Graphing)

In a world of DVDs and digital phones, are minerals really that useful? Discover with your students just how common and important minerals are with the following activity. Ask the children if they think they use minerals very often. Next, lead a discussion about how important and useful minerals are, giving several examples (gold and diamonds are used in jewelry, and graphite is used to make pencil lead). Then give each student a copy of page 28. Challenge each student to take the sheet home and look around the house to see if she can find one or more items made of each mineral listed on page 28. Instruct her to write the name of each item and draw an illustration of it in the appropriate section. Instruct students to return their papers to school the following day and share their findings. List each student's data on the board and have students total the number of items discovered for each category. They'll surely be surprised at the number of items discovered.

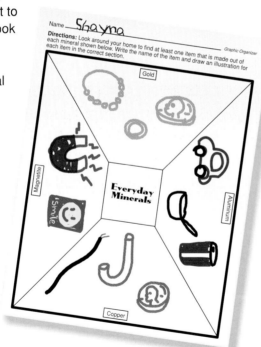

Background for the Teacher

- Rocks and minerals are used in many ways, from transportation and tools to art and medicine.
- Most rocks are a combination of different minerals.
- There are three kinds of rocks: *igneous, sedimentary,* and *metamorphic.*
- Most of the solid materials found on the earth are minerals.
- Each mineral occurs naturally, has a specific chemical makeup, and has atoms arranged in regular patterns, forming crystals.
- *Ore minerals* are processed to produce metals such as aluminum, zinc, and tin.
- *Precious metals,* such as gold and silver, have long been used to make coins and jewelry.
- *Gemstones*—such as diamonds, emeralds, and rubies—are minerals highly valued for their rarity and beauty.
- Some gemstones are important for their industrial uses. For example, diamonds are used in some drill bits and saws.

Reading About Rocks and Minerals

The Best Book of Fossils, Rocks, and Minerals by Chris Pellant (Kingfisher, 2000)
Everybody Needs a Rock by Byrd Baylor (Aladdin Paperbacks, 1987)
Rocks & Minerals (Eyewitness Books) by Dr. R. F. Symes (Dorling Kindersley Publishing, Inc.; 2000)
Rocks and Minerals (Eyewitness Explorers) by Steve Parker (Dorling Kindersley Publishing, Inc.; 1997)
Rocks & Minerals (The Wonders of Our World) by Neil Morris (Crabtree Publishing Company, 1998)

Art That Rocks!
(Art)

Make a splash with this creative art activity as your students use rocks to make paint! Explain to your students that, for thousands of years, people have crushed rocks to obtain a variety of colors for paints and dyes. Next, hold up a piece of white chalk and ask your students to name what you're holding. Tell your students that chalk is a soft white rock called limestone. Explain that chalk powder has long been used as a white pigment (coloring). Supply each student with the materials listed; then guide the student through the steps shown to make his own chalk painting. Display the completed paintings on a bulletin board titled "Art That Rocks!" Have students take their paintings home for display or use…maybe for future painting inspiration!

Materials for each student:
1 piece of white chalk
1 resealable plastic bag
glue-water solution (1 tbsp. white glue mixed with 1 tbsp. water)
newspaper
9" x 12" sheet of black construction paper
1 paintbrush
1 paper cup
1 plastic spoon
hammer

Steps:
1. Put your chalk inside a resealable plastic bag, flatten the bag to remove any extra air, and close the bag securely.
2. Place the bag in between layers of newspaper for cushioning.
3. Use a hammer to carefully crush the chalk into a powder.
4. Pour the chalk powder into a paper cup and add the glue solution. Mix thoroughly with a spoon.
5. Use the chalk paint and the paintbrush to create a picture on the black sheet of construction paper.

Rocks at Work
(Research, Matching)

Surprise! Did you know that rocks are hard at work all around us? Help your students make the connection between rocks and minerals and some commonly used items. Explain that ore minerals provide the metal for household appliances and cars, quartz is used in televisions and radios, and gypsum is used to make wallboard, plasterboard, and paint. Continue this connection with the following activity. In advance, set up a table with the following objects on it: a drill bit, a filled saltshaker, a lightbulb, a can of white paint, a container of bath powder, a glass, and a roll of film. Gather several reference books on rocks and minerals for student research. Then pair students and provide each pair with seven index cards, each labeled with one of the following rocks and minerals: diamond, halite, quartz, silver, talc, titanium, and tungsten. Tell pairs to research each rock or mineral to find its common use. Then have them match the rocks and minerals with the objects on display by placing the appropriate index card in front of the correct object. Afterward, ask students which match surprises them most. Throughout your study, encourage students to add to the display other products that have been made from rocks and minerals.

Rock Hounds
(Scavenger Hunt, Graphing)

Unleash your rock hounds for a fun family scavenger hunt! Send each student home with a copy of page 29. Explain that each student should recruit family members to help her locate and gather as many examples of rocks or minerals as she can in each category listed on page 29. Then remind students that many of the different kinds of rocks and minerals that they're looking for can be found right in their homes. (For example, a parent might have a ring that is made from a precious metal and a gemstone.) When students return to school with their lists, have each student read aloud the items found. Then make a chart of all the different rock and mineral items that are named. Use the chart to make a bar graph showing the rocks and minerals found by your students.

Munching on Minerals
(Cooking, Comparing by Taste, Writing)

Your dentist may shudder at the thought of your eating rocks, but did you know that you eat the mineral halite every day? Explain to students that halite is table salt. Then, using the simple biscuit recipe below, have them make two batches of biscuits—one with salt and one without. Have your students sample biscuits from each batch and compare. Instruct students to use page 30 to write down their observations. With this activity, your students will be able to taste the difference that minerals make in their lives.

Bite-Size Biscuits
(Makes one batch)

1/2 c. shortening
2 c. all-purpose flour
2 tsp. baking powder
1/2 tsp. salt
2/3 c. milk

Directions:
Heat your oven to 450°. Mix the shortening into the dry ingredients—flour, baking powder, and salt—with a fork until the mixture looks like small crumbs. Then stir in a little milk at a time until the dough leaves the side of the bowl and will make a ball.

Put the dough on a lightly floured surface. Knead it 20 to 25 times, for about 30 seconds. Then pat out the dough until it's a half inch thick. Cut the biscuits with the floured mouth of a clean baby food jar. Put the biscuits on an ungreased cookie sheet about one inch apart. Bake the biscuits for 12 to 14 minutes or until they're golden brown. Take the biscuits off the cookie sheet as soon as you pull them from the oven. Makes about 20 bite-size biscuits.

Strap on Your Tool Belts
(Discussion, Writing, Art)

For this activity, your students will need tool belts and their thinking caps. Have students use their imaginations to explore how people might have used rocks and minerals as tools. In advance, ask each student to bring a rock to class. Explain to students that before people had the technology to make tools from metal, they used rocks for tools. (In fact, a few groups in New Guinea and Australia still live as their Stone Age ancestors did long ago.) Then brainstorm with your class some of the ways they think rocks may have been used as tools. Write students' ideas on the board. Next, have them study the rocks they have brought to class, paying close attention to shape. What jobs listed would their rocks do best? Could their rocks do more than one job? Have students take a few minutes to imagine living without metal and having to use rocks as tools to complete everyday tasks. Then tell each student to write a story about how he might live without metal and draw a picture that shows him using his rock as a tool.

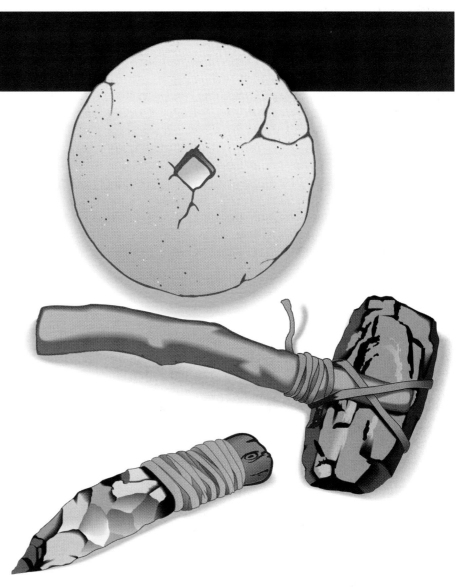

Stone Soup: An Old Tale
(Listening, Sequencing)

Marcia Brown's *Stone Soup: An Old Tale* (Aladdin Paperbacks, 1987) tells a story about three hungry soldiers who use stones to interest villagers in gladly giving what they were unwilling to give. The story can help children realize that the uses of rocks and minerals are limited only by their imaginations. After reading the book aloud, have each child cut out a large rock shape from a sheet of brown or gray construction paper. Have the child use a black marker to make the cutout look more rocklike. Next, provide a copy of page 31 for each student and instruct him to cut out the booklet pages on the bold lines. Have him personalize the front page and then sequentially number and stack the booklet pages. Direct him to staple the pages at the top and then glue the back of the last page to the front of his rock cutout as shown. Instruct the child to draw and color a picture on each booklet page to match the sentence. Display the completed booklets on a bulletin board titled "Stone Soup."

Name_____ *Graphic organizer*

Directions: Look around your home to find at least one item that is made out of each mineral shown below. Write the name of the item and draw an illustration for each item in the correct section.

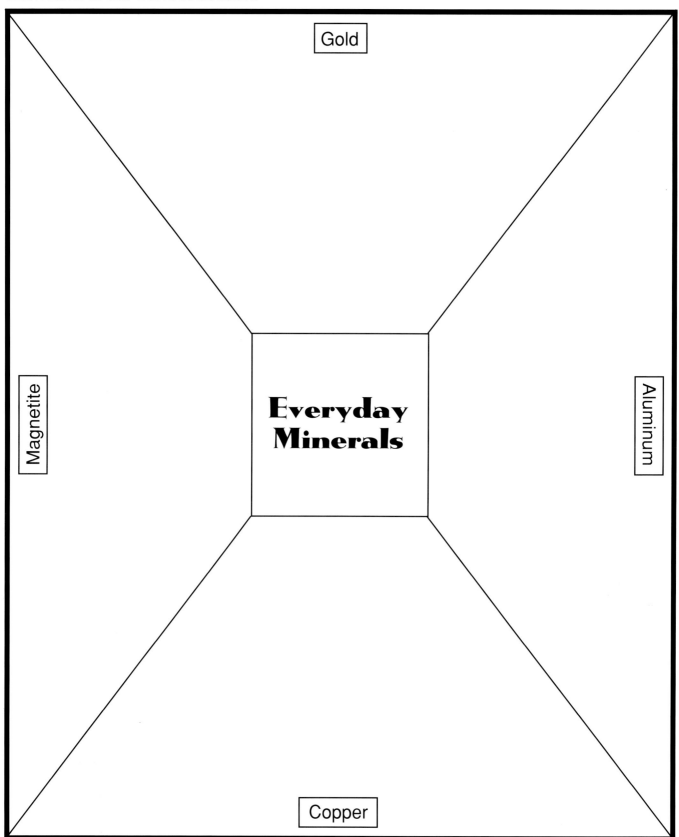

Gold

Magnetite

Everyday Minerals

Aluminum

Copper

©2000 The Education Center, Inc. • *Investigating Science* • *Rocks & Minerals* • TEC1747 • Key p. 48

Note to the teacher: Use with "Everyday Minerals" on page 24.

Rock Hounds

Directions: Have your family help you look around your home for items that come from or are made out of rocks and minerals. Try to find at least one item in each of the categories below. List the items in the appropriate spaces below. Amaze your classmates by sniffing out the most interesting and unusual items!

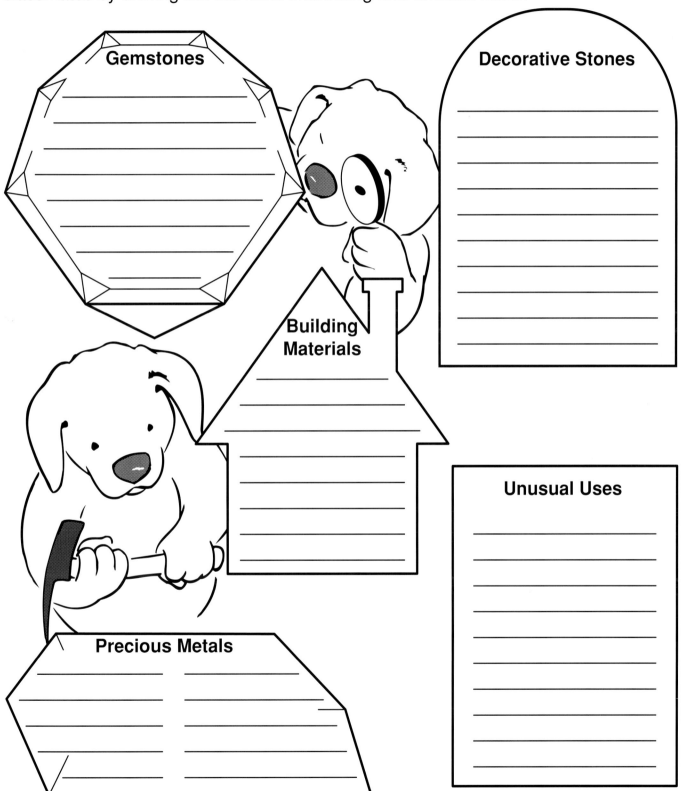

Gemstones

Decorative Stones

Building Materials

Unusual Uses

Precious Metals

Name_____

Munching on Minerals

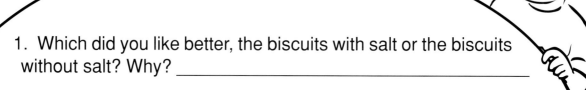

1. Which did you like better, the biscuits with salt or the biscuits without salt? Why? _____

_____

_____

_____

_____

2. Are there other foods that you think taste better either with or without salt? _____

_____

_____

_____

3. List other uses for salt. _____

_____

_____

_____

Note to the teacher: Use with "Munching on Minerals" on page 26.

Stone Soup: An Old Tale

_____
Name

The three soldiers sleep in the best beds in the village.

The villagers gather three round, smooth stones for the soldiers.

The villagers hide all of their food from the soldiers.

The villagers thank the soldiers for teaching them how to make soup from stones.

The soldiers make a soup fit for the king himself—from three stones.

Sand and Soil

Give your students the dirt on sand and soil with these great ideas, activities, and reproducibles!

The Dirt on Dirt
(Observing, Comparing)

Nitty-Gritty Literature

A Handful of Dirt by Raymond Bial (Walker Publishing Company, Inc.; 2000)

Mud Matters by Jennifer Owings Dewey (Marshall Cavendish, 1998)

Sand by Ellen J. Prager (National Geographic Society, 2000)

Your budding soil scientists may be surprised to learn that dirt is definitely not just dirt! Have students examine soil samples and they'll see for themselves. Divide the class into pairs and provide the materials listed for each twosome. Then guide each pair through the steps. After each pair completes its examination, provide time for students to discuss their findings.

Materials for each pair:
1 copy of page 36
1 cup of potting soil
1 cup of soil (collected locally)
1 cup of sand

3 paper plates
magnifying glass
marker

Steps:
1. Use a marker to label the border of each paper plate as shown. Then pour each soil or sand sample onto the appropriate plate.
2. Using the magnifying glass, carefully examine each sample.
3. Compare the size of the potting soil particles to the particles in the other two samples. Write a short description of the size of the potting soil particles in the appropriate box on page 36.
4. Compare the texture of the potting soil to the texture of the other two samples. Write a brief description of the potting soil's texture in the appropriate box.
5. Examine the potting soil for any organic materials (pieces of leaves, broken wood, or insects). Write a description of your findings in the appropriate box.
6. Describe the color of the potting soil in the appropriate box.
7. Repeat Steps 2–6 with the local soil sample and the sand.

Potting Soil

Sand

Local Soil

Background for the Teacher

- Soil is the product formed when rocks break down and mix with water, air, and rotting organic matter.
- Soil covers most of the world's land and its depth ranges from a few inches to hundreds of feet.
- Soil is made up of three basic *horizons,* or layers: *topsoil, subsoil,* and *bedrock.*
- There are as many as 70,000 kinds of soil in the United States. Some support plant growth better than others.
- There are five characteristics used to study soil: *texture, structure, porosity, color,* and *chemical composition.* Knowing these soil traits helps people plan how to best use their land.
- Texture is determined by the size of the particles in the soil.
- The structure of the soil is determined by the way the particles are arranged. For example, some soil particles clump together while other types of soil particles are granular and remain separate.
- The texture and structure help determine the porosity (number of spaces) of the soil. If the soil is too porous, water will drain too quickly, not allowing the water to reach the roots of plants.
- The color of the soil is determined by the different elements that the soil contains and how much *humus* (decomposing organic material) is in the soil. If the soil is too light and pale, fertilizers may be added.
- The chemical composition refers to whether the soil is *acidic, alkaline,* or *neutral.* Certain plants, such as cotton, grow better in acidic soil while other plants, such as grasses, grow better in alkaline soil.
- Sand consists of loose grains of minerals and rocks that are smaller than gravel but larger than silt.
- Among other things, sand is used to make concrete, to clean buildings, and to provide traction on ice.

Soil Formation
(Making a Booklet, Sequencing)

Just where does soil come from? To answer this question and give your students the scoop on soil formation, have them complete the following booklet project! To begin, introduce your students to the process that turns rock into soil by reading *The Mountain That Loved a Bird* by Alice McLerran (Aladdin Paperbacks, 2000). After reading, have students discuss the changes that took place in the mountain. Follow up the discussion by having each student make a soil formation booklet. Give each child a copy of page 37 and five 4¹⁄₂" x 6" pieces of construction paper, crayons, glue, and scissors. Instruct the student to color and cut out the picture and description cards on page 37. Next, direct her to glue each picture card to the top of a different 4¹⁄₂" x 6" piece of construction paper. Then have her find the matching description card and glue it below the appropriate picture. To create a cover for the booklet, instruct the student to title the fifth piece of construction paper "Soil Is Formed!" Then have her decorate the cover as desired. Next, have the student stack the five pages in sequential order with the cover on top. Direct her to staple the booklet along the left-hand side. Encourage each student to take her booklet home and share her knowledge of soil formation with her family.

The Search for Suitable Soil
(Making a Science Journal, Experiment)

Determining which soil is best suited for supporting plant growth is as easy as 1, 2, 3 with this activity! In advance, give each student one copy of the cover pattern on page 38 and five copies of the journal page pattern on page 38. Have the student personalize, decorate, and cut out the cover. Then have him cut out each journal page. Next, direct him to stack the pages with the cover on top and staple them together to form a science journal. To begin the experiment, divide the class into small groups and provide the materials listed. Guide your students through the steps shown to help them discover whether potting soil, local soil, or sand is best for growing grass. On the 15th day of the experiment, have each group share its findings and state which sample (potting soil, local soil, sand) was best for growing grass.

Materials for each group:

3 plastic cups	gravel	permanent black marker
potting soil	grass seed	spoon
soil (collected locally)	water	pencil (sharpened)
sand		

Steps:
1. Use a permanent marker to label the three cups as shown.
2. Pour a layer of gravel into the bottom of each cup.
3. Fill each cup three-fourths full of the appropriate material.
4. Sprinkle a spoonful of grass seed on top of each cup. Use the point of a pencil to gently cover the seeds with sand or soil.
5. Use the spoon to gently water the seeds in each cup. Place the cups in a sunny location. Water the seeds every other day throughout the experiment.
6. Every three days examine the progress of the seeds in each cup. Record your observations on a page in your science journal. Continue observing the cups and recording data for a total of 15 days.
7. As a group, evaluate your observations and decide which sample was best for growing grass seed.

Passing the Acid Test
(Experiment)

Introduce your students to the chemical composition of soil with the following exploration. Explain to students that different soil samples can have different chemical compositions. Some plants thrive in soil that is less acidic while other plants grow well in soil that is more acidic. Further explain that determining the chemical composition of soil helps farmers decide which crops to plant.

In advance, collect soil samples from five different locations. (These locations can be from different areas of the school grounds or from locations such as your yard, the beach, a field, etc.) To begin the exploration, divide your students into small groups. Give each group the materials listed and have them follow the steps to complete the experiment. After completing the experiment, have students discuss possible reasons why some of the soil samples were more acidic than others.

Materials for each group:
5 clear plastic cups
5 soil samples, each from a different location
blue litmus paper strips
eyedropper
water
permanent black marker
spoon

Steps:
1. Use a marker to label each cup with the location at which the soil was found.
2. Place one litmus strip in the bottom of each cup.
3. Pour two spoonfuls of each soil sample into the appropriately labeled cup on top of the litmus strip.
4. Lift one cup until the bottom of the cup is visible. Using the eyedropper, drip water onto the soil until it soaks through and the strip appears to be wet.
5. Watch the strip and note any color change. If the sample is acidic, the strip will turn pink. Record your findings for each cup on a sheet of paper.

A Sensational Soaking Race
(Experiment)

Ready, set, soak! Which type of soil soaks up water the fastest? Have your students help you conduct this outdoor experiment to find out. Explain to students that plants need to have moist soil to grow. Also, topsoil must be able to hold water so that rain or floodwater doesn't wash away the richest topsoil. Gather the materials listed and follow the steps to find soil that is able to hold water.

Materials:
1 copy of page 39 for each student
4 cans, each the same size
    with the tops and bottoms removed
measuring cup
water
stopwatch or watch with a second hand

Steps:
1. Select four outdoor locations to test (playground, school garden, nearby woods, etc.). Push one can halfway into the soil at each location. Take students on a short tour, show them the locations, and have each child draw the locations on page 39.
2. Explain that at each location a cup of water will be poured into each can. Then have each child predict which location will absorb the water the quickest and which locations will absorb the water more slowly. Have the student record his prediction on page 39.
3. Direct a student to pour one cup of water into the can at location 1. As soon as the student pours the water, begin timing the absorption. Have students record the amount of time it takes for the water to be completely absorbed.
4. Repeat the process at each of the remaining three locations.
5. Return to the classroom and have students use the recorded absorption times at each location to help them complete the bottom of page 39. Provide time for each child to share his conclusions with the class (some areas may have different types of soil such as sand or clay, while others may have already been damp due to being in a wet or shady area).

Shake Up Some Sand!
(Experiment)

Get ready to shake, shake, shake with this sand-making activity. Explain to students that some sand is made of rock fragments and seashells that have been broken down by the crashing waves of the sea. Next, tell your students that they are going to create their own sand. Divide your students into pairs; then provide each pair with the materials listed below. Guide each pair through the steps below to create the sand.

Materials for each pair of students:

1 plastic container with a lid
3–5 small clean pebbles
3–5 small clean seashells

water
magnifying glass
paper towels

Steps:
1. Place the pebbles and shells inside the plastic container.
2. Pour in enough water to cover the shells and pebbles.
3. Secure the lid tightly on the container.
4. Vigorously shake the container for two minutes; then have your partner shake the container for two minutes.
5. Place the container on a flat surface and remove the lid. Observe the water in the container. *(The water will be cloudy.)* Explain why the water looks as it does. *(During the shaking, tiny bits broke off the shells and pebbles.)*
6. Remove the shells and pebbles and place them on paper towels. Observe them with the magnifying glass. What do they look like? *(Students may notice tiny nicks and crannies caused by the shaking.)*
7. Carefully run your fingers along the bottom of the plastic container. What do you notice? *(It feels gritty.)*
8. What do you think will happen if you put the pebbles and shells back into the container, replace the lid, and continue to shake? *(More grains of sand will form at the bottom of the container.)*

Putting Sand to Work
(Experiment)

There are many uses for sand! Have your students make a piece of sandpaper to get a firsthand look at one of the uses of sand. Explain to students that sand is mixed with cement to build sidewalks and walls, sprinkled on icy roads to give cars traction, blown at buildings to clean bricks and stones, and put in sandbags to hold back water. Further explain that sand is also used to make sandpaper. Give each child one 3¹/₂" x 2¹/₂" piece of construction paper, one-fourth cup of sand, glue, and a paint-brush. Have the student paint a thin layer of glue on one side of the construction paper. Then direct her to sprinkle the sand over the glue and shake the excess off over a trash can. Once the glue has dried, invite each child to remove the paint from one of her pencils by rubbing it with her sandpaper. As children work, encourage them to notice that the sandpaper makes the wood feel smooth. Have children brainstorm uses for sandpaper. With this activity, students are sure to discover that sand is very useful!

Name _____

36

Examine It!

Potting Soil

Local Soil

Sand

	Particle Size	Texture	Organic Material	Color
Potting Soil				
Local Soil				
Sand				

Note to the teacher: Use with "The Dirt on Dirt" on page 32.

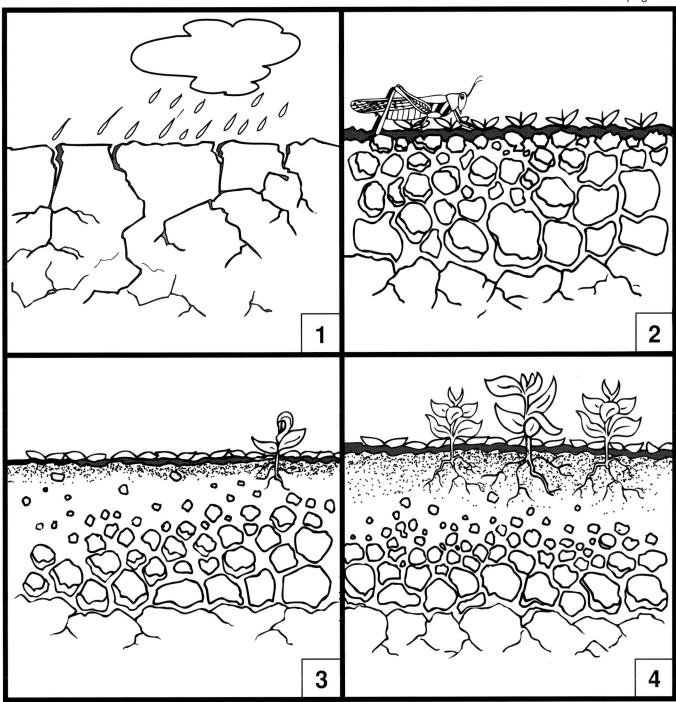

Finally, the soil is healthy and able to grow plants.

Soil begins to form when weather and other natural forces break down rocks and other substances.

Once the rocks begin to break down, plantlike matter and animal matter help them continue to break down.

Different layers, or *horizons,* begin to show in the soil.

Patterns

Use with "The Search for Suitable Soil" on page 33.

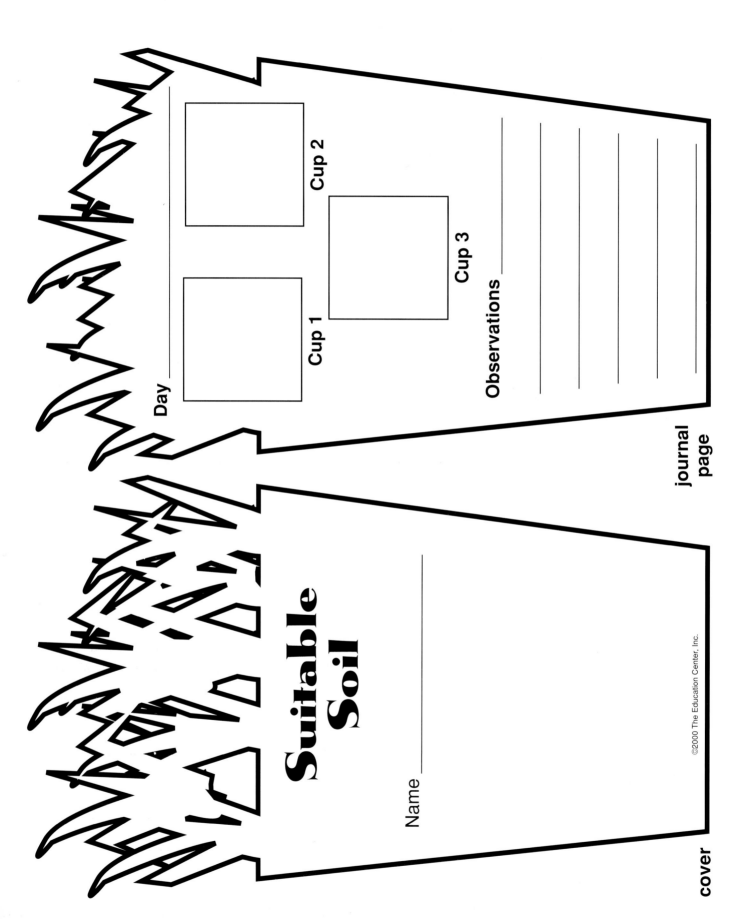

Day

Cup 1

Cup 2

Cup 3

Observations

journal page

Suitable Soil

Name

cover

©2000 The Education Center, Inc. • *Investigating Science • Rocks & Minerals* • TEC1747

Name _____ *Experiment*

A Sensational Soaking Race

Draw a picture of each location in the appropriate box.

Predict what will happen: _____

_____

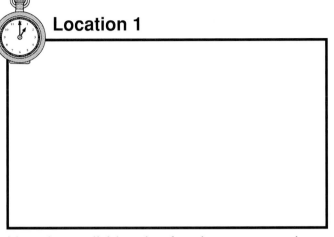 **Location 1**

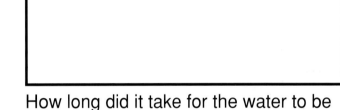 **Location 2**

How long did it take for the water to be completely absorbed? _____

How long did it take for the water to be completely absorbed? _____

 **Location 3**

 **Location 4**

How long did it take for the water to be completely absorbed? _____

How long did it take for the water to be completely absorbed? _____

Which location soaked up the water the quickest? _____

Which location soaked up the water the slowest? _____

What conclusions can you make? _____

_____

_____

Note to the teacher: Use with "A Sensational Soaking Race" on page 34.

Famous and Unusual Rocks

Majestic…grand…and mysterious. Use the following activities to teach your students about some fascinating natural and man-made rock formations.

Steady hands and lots of rocks are all that's needed to stack up balance skills with this construction activity! In advance, ask each child to bring a variety of rocks from home. Place all of the rocks in four different containers. Divide your students into four small groups and give each group a container of rocks. Next, explain to students that there are many rock formations made up of towers of balancing boulders (such as Balanced Rock in Colorado Springs, Colorado). Ask each group to experiment with different-sized rocks to create a rock sculpture. If desired, have each group test the steadiness of its sculpture by placing small objects on top of it. Later, gather students together to discuss the different methods they used to create strong and stable sculptures. Rock on!

Background for the Teacher

- Eight elements make up more than 98% of all the rocks in the world: *oxygen, silicon, aluminum, iron, calcium, sodium, potassium,* and *magnesium*.
- *Balanced Rock* is an enormous sandstone block balanced on a small base near Colorado Springs, Colorado.
- Thin slabs of *itacolumite,* a rare kind of sandstone found in India and North Carolina, can be bent by hand.
- *Pumice,* a volcanic rock, floats on water.
- *Extrusive rocks* form when magma is forced out onto the earth's surface.
- *Intrusive rocks* form when magma does not rise all the way to the earth's surface.
- *Erosion* is a natural process by which rock and soil are broken away from the earth's surface and moved to another area.
- *Mount Rushmore National Memorial* in South Dakota took more than 14 years to complete. The sculpted head of George Washington is as high as a five-story building. If the head were part of a real person, that person would be 465 feet tall!
- The *Grand Canyon,* which goes through northwestern Arizona, extends 277 miles and is about one mile deep.
- *Devils Tower National Monument,* an 865-foot-tall rock column in northeastern Wyoming, was made famous by the movie *Close Encounters of the Third Kind.*
- *Stonehenge,* in southwestern England, is made up of huge cut stones arranged in circles.

Boulder Books

America's Top 10 Natural Wonders by Edward Ricciuti (Blackbirch Marketing, 1998)

The Big Rock by Bruce Hiscock (Aladdin Paperbacks, 1999)

Grand Canyon: Exploring a Natural Wonder by Wendell Minor (Scholastic Inc., 1998)

The Pebble in My Pocket: A History of Our Earth by Meredith Hooper (Viking Children's Books, 1996)

Volcanoes! Mountains of Fire by Eric Arnold (Random House, Inc.; 1997)

A Yellowstone ABC by Cyd Martin (Roberts Rinehart Pub., 1992)

Finding Fossils
(Natural Rock Formations, Completing a Diagram)

After investigating this slice of ancient rock, your students will see how the Grand Canyon provides a record of the earth's history. In advance, make a copy of page 45 for each student. Explain to students that the Grand Canyon (in Arizona) is one of the most famous scenic wonders in the United States because of its age and immense size. Further explain that billions of years ago, the rocks at the bottom of the Grand Canyon were an ocean floor. Over the years, layers of sandstone, shale, and limestone have built up on top of the floor. Over time, the rushing water of the Colorado River has worn away the stone, revealing the changes that have occurred in the earth's surface over the last two billion years and fossils hidden in the canyon's rocks. Give each child a copy of page 45 and have him follow the directions for completing the activity.

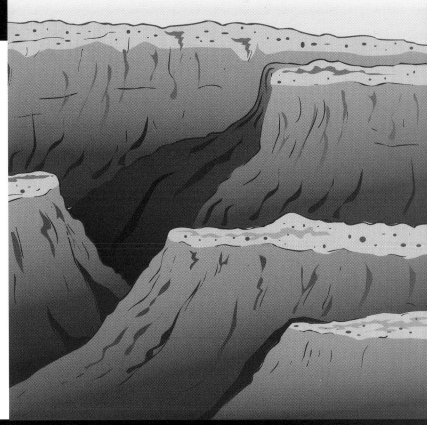

Water Power
(Natural Rock Formations, Simulation)

Your students will rush to experiment with the following time-lapsed version of water *erosion*. In advance, fill two resealable plastic sandwich bags with water (add food coloring if desired), and place them in a freezer overnight. Also collect a large aluminum baking pan and an empty plastic squirt bottle, such as a liquid detergent container. Explain to students that the beautiful landscape of the Grand Canyon is the world's most dramatic example of water erosion. Further explain that the Colorado River formed the canyon over millions of years as it wore down layers of rock.

To demonstrate water erosion, remove the colored ice from the freezer bags and place the two chunks of ice (representing rocks) side by side in the baking pan. Fill the bottle with water; then have a volunteer squirt it between the rocks to represent rushing water. Experiment with warm water and cool water. Ask your students to observe the changes that occur. Discuss how this experiment compares with the wearing away of rock by water.

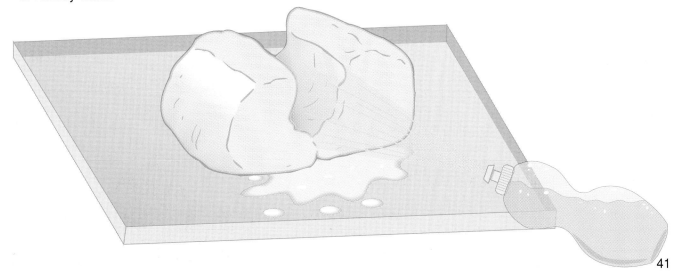

41

Rainbow Replica
(Natural Rock Formations, Creative Writing)

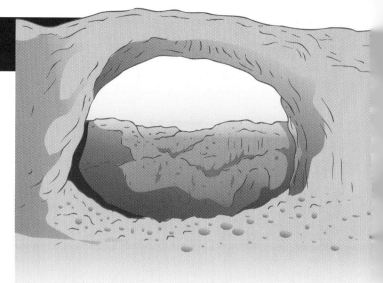

Intrigue your students by telling them there are Native American legends associated with many natural wonders. Explain to students that there are three huge natural sandstone bridges located in Utah. Rainbow Bridge, which arches 290 feet above the Glen Canyon floor, is the largest known natural stone bridge in the world. Ask students to think about how Rainbow Bridge may have been formed. Then have each student write a legend that describes her idea. After they share their stories, tell students that Native American legends explain Rainbow Bridge as an actual rainbow that turned into stone. Also tell them that scientists believe it was formed by water erosion.

Tallest Tower
(Natural Rock Formations, Demonstration)

The following simple simulation demonstrates how one rock wonder was formed. To prepare, place a tall wooden block in a plastic tub and completely cover it with sand to create a hill. Also fill a watering can with water. Tell your students that deep within the earth there are places where rock has melted into *magma.* When magma erupts out of the earth through a volcano, it's called *lava.* Explain that Devils Tower in Wyoming (the tallest rock formation of its type in America) was formed when magma was forced up inside a volcano, but then did *not* erupt out the top. Instead, the magma cooled and hardened underground. Erosion eventually revealed the rock tower. To begin, tell students the sand hill represents the soft rock that surrounded Devils Tower. Then slowly sprinkle water onto the sand to reveal the tower buried within it. Ask students to observe the changes and compare them to the erosion that revealed Devils Tower.

Magma Munch
(Recipe)

Your students will enjoy this crunchy, munchy magma treat!

Ingredients and utensils:

4 tbsp. corn syrup
$1/2$ c. white sugar
2 tbsp. baking soda
saucepan

wooden spoon
aluminum pan
cooking spray

Steps for the teacher:
1. Spray the aluminum pan with cooking spray and set it aside.
2. Cook the corn syrup and sugar in the saucepan over medium heat, stirring constantly until it boils. Boil the "magma" for seven minutes.
3. Remove the saucepan from the heat and quickly stir in the baking soda until the magma is foamy.
4. Use the wooden spoon to pour the magma into the prepared pan and allow it to cool for ten minutes. Then break into pieces.

Memorable Designs
(Man-Made Rock Formations, Creating an Original Design)

The following memorable experience will be etched in the minds of your students. In advance, make a copy of page 46 for each student. Explain to your students that Mount Rushmore National Memorial, located in the Black Hills of South Dakota, is a huge granite carving of the faces of four American presidents: George Washington, Thomas Jefferson, Theodore Roosevelt, and Abraham Lincoln. Further explain that workers sculpted the faces into the cliff using drills and dynamite.

Ask students what they think the word *memorial* means. Then brainstorm with them people or places in your area that students think should be *memorialized*. Next, give each student a copy of page 46. Have him choose a person or place to be the subject for a memorial. Instruct each student to complete the page by drawing his design for the memorial and then writing a paragraph about it.

Larger Than Life
(Man-Made Rock Formations, Research, Art)

Your students will dig into sculpting with the following hands-on activity! In advance, obtain one block of floral foam (or plastic foam) and one plastic spoon for each child. Explain to students that Stone Mountain (near Atlanta, Georgia) has huge granite carvings of Civil War figures Jefferson Davis, Robert E. Lee, and Stonewall Jackson. Challenge your students to read about Stone Mountain and Mount Rushmore to discover what the two have in common. *(Gutzon Borglum was the first sculptor to work on the Stone Mountain monument. He left it to work on the Mount Rushmore carvings.)* Discuss with students how each monument was constructed. Then give each child a block of foam and a plastic spoon and have him sculpt his own monument. Or suggest that he sculpt his design from "Memorable Designs" above.

Sensational Circle
(Mysterious Rock Formations, Making a Model)

Challenge your students' balancing skills as they re-create a mysterious rock formation. In advance, collect several sets of dominoes and make a copy of page 47 for each child. Explain to students that *Stonehenge,* located in England, is an ancient monument made up of many huge cut stones set in a circle. Further explain that some scientists believe Stonehenge was an ancient calendar. Then divide students into small groups and give each group a supply of dominoes and give each student a copy of page 47. Ask each group to create a formation similar to the Stonehenge model. Ask students to think about how Stonehenge may have been created. Then have each student write his explanation in the space provided on page 47.

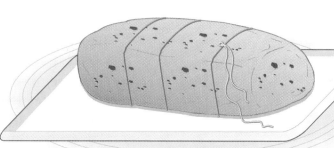

Magnificent Movers
(Mysterious Rock Formations, Simple Machines, Experimentation)

Your students will discover that sometimes a simple idea can help move mountains—or huge stones!—with the following hands-on activity. To prepare, collect six pencils, a medium-sized stone or wooden block, a clean Styrofoam® meat tray, a dish tub of water, and a length of string for each small group. Each group will also need a sheet of ice. (Freeze baking pans filled with water.) Tell students there are several ideas to explain how huge stones were moved to create Stonehenge. Those methods include rolling the stones across logs on the ground, floating the stones on rafts in the water, and pulling them across ice in the winter.

Next, divide students into small groups and give each group the needed supplies. Have each group tie the string around its stone; then direct each group to experiment with the three methods of moving the stone: rolling it on the pencils; floating it on a raft (meat tray) in the tub of water; and pulling it over ice. Later, gather all your students and have each group demonstrate the method it believes was the best.

Grand Layers of Rock

Find and color each fossil hidden in a layer of rock.
Color each rock layer. Use the key at the bottom of the page.
Use the key to help you label each rock layer in the blank provided.

shark teeth   (limestone)

clams   (limestone)

scorpion tracks   (sandstone)

reptile tracks   (sandstone)

insect wings   (shale)

land plants   (shale)

ferns   (shale or sandstone)

snails   (shale or sandstone)

later shelled animals   (limestone)

bony fish plates   (limestone)

sea creatures   (shale)

earlier shelled animals   (shale)

Key
limestone = gray
sandstone = yellow
shale = brown
shale or sandstone = red

Note to the teacher: Use with "Finding Fossils" on page 41.

A Memorable Design

Think of a person or a place that deserves a memorial.
Draw your original design for the memorial in the box below.
Then write a paragraph about your memorial.

_____
_____
_____
_____
_____

Circle of Stone

Thirty stones once stood in the outer ring of Stonehenge. A ring of smaller stones was placed on top of the 30 standing stones.

Draw four stone pillars to complete the diagram.

Use 30 dominoes to create a model of Stonehenge's outer ring. Then place a ring of dominoes flat on top of the standing dominoes.

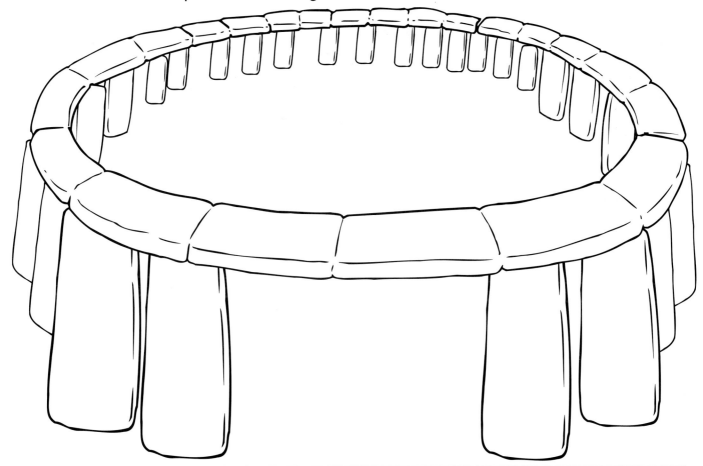

Write about it: How hard was it to construct your model? Did you knock down any dominoes? Imagine what it must have been like to move the 30 blocks weighing about 28 tons each! Tell how you think the stones were placed upright to make the circle of Stonehenge.

_____

_____

_____

_____

_____

_____

©2000 The Education Center, Inc. • *Investigating Science* • *Rocks & Minerals* • TEC1747

Answer Keys

Page 17
1. Igneous rock forms when magma cools and hardens.
2. Basalt is the most common igneous rock.
3. Sedimentary rock forms from layers of sediment.
4. Sandstone is one type of sedimentary rock.
5. Metamorphic rock forms when rocks are changed by heat and/or pressure.
6. Marble is a type of metamorphic rock.

Pages 18 and 19
Igneous Rock—This type of rock forms when molten material, or magma, cools and hardens.
Metamorphic Rock—This type of rock forms when heat or pressure or both cause changes in the other two types of rocks.
Sedimentary Rock—This type of rock forms when small pieces of clay, silt, or sand settle into layers on the bottoms of lakes and oceans. The pressure of the water and the layers above compress the pieces into rock.

Page 23
1. Igneous
2. Sedimentary
3. Metamorphic

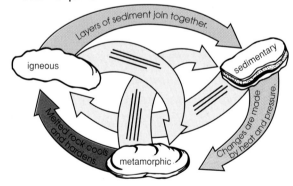

Page 28
Answers will vary. Possible answers include the following:
Gold—necklaces, rings
Aluminum—cars, pots and pans, soft drink cans
Copper—coins, plumbing pipes, electrical wires
Magnetite—magnets, refrigerator magnets

Page 31
Title Page
Page 1: The villagers hide all of their food from the soldiers.
Page 2: The villagers gather three round, smooth stones for the soldiers.
Page 3: The soldiers make a soup fit for the king himself—from three stones.
Page 4: The three soldiers sleep in the best beds in the village.
Page 5: The villagers thank the soldiers for teaching them how to make soup from stones.

Page 45

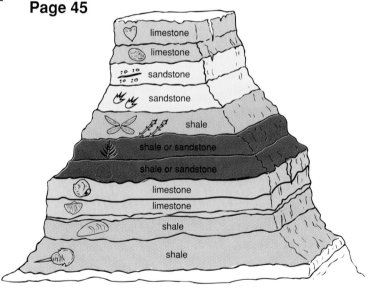

Page 37

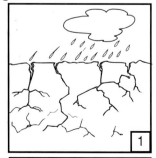
Soil begins to form when weather and other natural forces break down rocks and other substances.

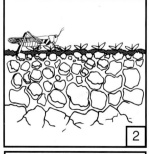
Once the rocks begin to break down, plantlike matter and animal matter help them continue to break down.

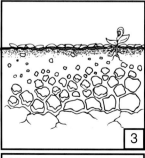
Different layers, or *horizons*, begin to show in the soil.

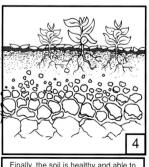
Finally, the soil is healthy and able to grow plants.